George Washington Wasn't Always Old

George Washington Wasn't Always Old

by Alice Fleming
illustrated by Bert Dodson

SIMON & SCHUSTER BOOKS FOR YOUNG READERS
Published by Simon & Schuster
New York • London • Toronto • Sydney • Tokyo • Singapore

SIMON & SCHUSTER BOOKS FOR YOUNG READERS
Simon & Schuster Building, Rockefeller Center
1230 Avenue of the Americas, New York, New York 10020
Text copyright © 1991 by Alice Fleming. Illustrations copyright © 1991
by Bert Dodson. All rights reserved including the right of reproduction in
whole or in part in any form. SIMON & SCHUSTER BOOKS FOR
YOUNG READERS is a trademark of Simon & Schuster.

Designed by Lucille Chomowicz
Manufactured in the United States of America 10 9 8 7 6 5 4 3 2 1

Library of Congress Cataloging-in-Publication Data
Fleming, Alice Mulcahey, 1928-   George Washington wasn't always old /
by Alice Fleming ; illustrated by Bert Dodson. Summary: Presents the
boyhood life of George Washington up to his twenty-first birthday.
1. Washington, George, 1732-1799—Juvenile literature.
2. President—United States—Biography—Juvenile literature.
3. Generals—United States—Biography—Juvenile literature.
[1. Washington, George, 1732-1799. 2. Presidents.] I. Dodson, Bert, ill.
II. Title. E312.66.F54   1991   973.4'1'092—dc20   [B]   [92]
90-10043   ISBN 0-671-69557-6

For Noah — AF

To Ann Wigmore, a contemporary American hero — BD

1

You probably won't believe this — hardly anyone does — but George Washington wasn't always old. Once upon a time, he was young enough to turn somersaults and tease his little sister and throw tantrums when he couldn't have his own way.

George Washington wasn't anybody special then — just a boy with blue eyes and reddish-brown hair who lived on a farm in the British colony of Virginia. His family wasn't very special either. His father, Augustine Washington, ran an ironworks and raised tobacco; his mother, Mary, ran the house and helped raise the children.

It never occurred to the Washingtons that one of

those children might grow up to be the first President of the United States. Why should it? There wasn't any United States back then. If you'd mentioned the name, people would have said, "The United what?" or "Huh?" or — if they really weren't paying attention — "No thank you, I never eat grapes."

George Washington was born around ten o'clock one winter morning. His birthday was recorded in the family Bible as February 11, 1731. About twenty years later, Great Britain and her colonies switched from the Old Style to the New Style calendar and George got a new birthday: February 22, 1732.

For the first few years of his life, George lived in a brick cottage in Westmoreland County, a few miles from what is now the town of Oak Grove in the state of Virginia.

Back then, there weren't any cities or towns in Westmoreland County. There weren't any streets or avenues either. A family's address was either the name of the farm they lived on — Longwood or Rosewell or Gunston — or how a stranger might find it — "just past the gristmill" or "a mile beyond the church." The Washingtons' address was "on Pope's Creek not far from the Potomac River."

When George was about three years old, his father

decided to lease the farm on Pope's Creek to tenant farmers, and move to another farm about forty miles up the river. This one had a name: Epsewasson.

There were a couple of trails that led to the upper Potomac but they weren't wide enough for a wagonload of furniture to squeeze by. Even if they had been, there were so many creeks and inlets and marshes along the way that the driver would have spent half his time coaxing his horses on and off ferries, and the other half digging his wheels out of the mud.

The best way for the Washingtons to move their belongings from Pope's Creek to Epsewasson was the same way Virginians moved anything that couldn't be carried in their arms or stuffed into their saddle bags — by boat.

Mary Washington instructed the house slaves to pack up the dishes, roll up the bedding, and fold up everyone's clothes. Then they loaded everything onto a fleet of long barges and rowed them up the river to Epsewasson.

Unpacking and getting settled in a new house was as much of a hassle in the eighteenth century as it is in the twentieth. There were the usual searches for missing items: Has anybody seen the candle snuffer? Where did the tea caddy go?

And there were the usual worries about where to put the furniture: Did the tilt-top table look better here — or there? Should the leather armchair go to the left — or the right — of the fireplace?

Eventually, George's mother was satisfied that nothing had been lost or left behind, and that every piece of furniture had been placed exactly where it belonged. By that time Epsewasson had stopped feeling like a new house and began to feel like home.

George's father had bought a choice piece of land — 2500 acres fronting on the Potomac — but it wasn't in a choice location. Epsewasson was so far up the river it was practically in the wilderness. People nowadays would call it the boondocks.

George didn't care. Until then he had spent most of his time learning to walk and talk and tell the difference between horses and cows and drink his breakfast chocolate without dribbling too much of it down his chin. Now he was ready to take an interest in the world around him and, for a small boy, Epsewasson was a very interesting world. It had fields to romp in and haystacks to jump in. There were horses in the stables, chickens in the barnyard and crabs scurrying across the mud flats at low tide.

George had only one complaint about Epsewasson: his father wasn't around as much as he'd like. He'd been told why. His father had to spend more time at the ironworks. Why? Because the manager had died and there wasn't anyone else to run it. Why? Because there wasn't, George, that's why.

If George was upset because his father spent two or three days a week at the ironworks, you can imagine how he felt when his father announced that he had to go to London. That could, and did, take half a year. Augustine Washington sailed off in the middle of winter and didn't return until the following summer. Somehow, George survived.

The trip had something to do with the ironworks, but George wasn't sure exactly what. He did know that his father's visit to England had given him a chance to see his sons from his first marriage, Lawrence and Austin (who was really Augustine, Jr.). They had been sent off to the Appleby School after their mother died and their father remarried, a year or so before George was born.

George was anxious to find out more about these two half-brothers he had heard about but never met. What did they do at Appleby besides study? Had they

ever met King George? When would they come home?
Could he go to Appleby someday too?

The answer to the last question was: "We'll see."
The answer to the others was: Lawrence would be
home in a few more months. George could ask him in
person.

Lawrence's ship dropped anchor in the Potomac River one balmy day and, before long, he was waving to his family from the stern of the skiff that a burly young sailor was rowing towards shore.

A few minutes later, Lawrence was hugging his father and stepmother and being introduced to a whole tribe of younger Washingtons. By this time George had a sister, Betty, and three brothers — Samuel, John Augustine (who was usually called Jack) and Charles.

The next order of business was showing Lawrence around Epsewasson. As his father was quick to point out, the house wasn't much but the land was superb. Who cared if it was a little bit out of the way? People would start moving to the upper Potomac before too long. When that happened, Epsewasson would be worth twice as much as he'd paid for it.

Like most six-year-olds, George wasn't particularly interested in the grownups' talk about land. What he was interested in, and fascinated by, was the twenty-year-old half-brother he had finally met.

Lawrence was friendly and easy-going and, unlike George, he always seemed to know exactly what to do and say. What pleased George most was that Lawrence liked him, too.

George would have been happy to have Lawrence stay with them forever, but he was old enough to be out on his own. Besides, Augustine Washingon had a plan. He was tired of traveling back and forth to the ironworks. If Lawrence stayed at Epsewasson, his father and stepmother could find a place that wasn't so far away.

A few weeks later, George's father spied an ad in the *Virginia Gazette* for a farm that was an easy ride from the ironworks. It stood on a bluff overlooking the Rappahannock River and, because there was a ferry landing at the bottom of the bluff, the place was called Ferry Farm.

In some ways, Ferry Farm wasn't much different

from Epsewasson. It had the same crops in the fields, the same horses and cows in the pasture, the same pigs and chickens in the barnyard. The one big difference was that Ferry Farm wasn't in the boondocks. It was only a ferryboat ride away from a town.

The town was Fredericksburg. It had been laid out the year George II became King of England — 1727 — and named after his eldest son, Frederick, the Prince of Wales.

A visitor who had been to London or Philadelphia or even Williamsburg might have turned up his nose at the tiny town but to George, who had spent his entire life on farms, Fredericksburg was a world of wonders. It had shops that sold everything from shoe buckles to sugar candy, and a wharf where sea captains compared notes on the winds and the tides, and traded their cargoes of fine clothes and furniture from London for casks of choice Virginia tobacco.

About two months after the Washingtons moved to Ferry Farm, George celebrated his seventh birthday. There might have been a hatchet among his presents and he might have used it to chop down one of the trees in his father's cherry orchard. It's possible that when his father came storming in demanding to know what happened, George decided it would be better to tell the truth and blurted out the whole story.

Then again that could have happened at some other time or — it may not have happened at all. Some people think it didn't, and that the story was made up years later to show boys and girls how perfect George Washington was — which he wasn't, of course. Nobody is.

One thing you can be sure of though, is that even at the age of seven, George was showing signs of being tall. His legs always seemed to be too long for his breeches, his toes ready to pop through the tips of his shoes. George didn't mind. The bigger he got the more chance there was that his mother would stop treating him like a baby.

Although Mary Washington had five children to worry about, the one she worried about most was George. When he sat on a fence she said, "Don't fall off." When he shinnied up a tree she said, "Don't fall down." When he headed for the river she said, "Don't fall in."

George tried to convince her he was old enough to take care of himself. His father said so, too, but Mary Washington couldn't stop worrying. Luckily, George had Epsewasson to escape to. Lawrence had told him to come back for a visit whenever he pleased.

George loved visiting Lawrence. Now that he was tall enough to ride a horse without slipping out of the saddle, they went for early morning rides around the farm. Breakfast would be waiting when they returned — plates heaped high with ham, dried venison, warm bread and butter, and a pot of hot chocolate to wash it all down.

Managing Epsewasson took up most of Lawrence's day. He had to make sure the house and barns were in good repair, and that the crops, livestock and slaves

were as healthy as they could be. Like most sensible planters, the Washingtons took good care of their slaves — not only because they cost money, but because it was impossible to run a plantation without them.

Whether the Washingtons and their fellow planters ever stopped to consider what a dreadful system slavery was is another question. Chances are they didn't but if they did, they probably said "Yes, but . . ." the way people do when they're doing something wrong, and know it, but don't want to stop.

Lawrence and George talked about farming and

horses — George loved horses — and about Epsewasson and Ferry Farm and Virginia and England and Appleby. They got along so well, it was hard to believe there was almost fifteen years difference in their ages.

If anyone had asked George who he cared about most in the world, his answer would have been Lawrence. And if anyone had asked Lawrence the same question, his answer almost surely would have been George.

3

George's parents moved to Ferry Farm because it was close to the ironworks, but they must have been glad to be close to Fredericksburg as well. They had five children to educate, and the town had a brand new school.

The school had been started by the Rev. Mr. James Marye, the rector of St. George's Church. It cost money to go there so not everybody went. There were only about a dozen students and instead of being divided into grades, they met in a single classroom. The Rev. Mr. Marye took them one or two at a time and taught them whatever they were ready to learn.

George was looking forward to school. He already knew his letters and his numbers but he wanted to learn how to write as gracefully as his father and to read well enough to enjoy the books in Lawrence's library. His only worry was whether he'd still have time to visit Epsewasson. By now, it was his second home.

As it turned out, there weren't going to be too many more visits anyway. Lawrence was leaving Epsewasson to join the army.

In the fall of 1739 England declared war against Spain. The war started because a British sea captain named Robert Jenkins had his ear lopped off by some Spanish coastguardsmen patrolling the Caribbean Sea. The coastguardsmen were trying to stop English ships from trading with the Spanish colonies in Latin America. Spain wanted all the business for herself.

The English didn't expect to have any trouble winning the War of Jenkins's Ear (it sounded silly but that's what they called it). A British fleet commanded by Admiral Edward Vernon had already scored a great victory. They swooped into the harbor of Porto Bello in Panama and captured the town within forty-eight hours.

According to the reports from London, Admiral Vernon was preparing for another attack. The War

Office was going to give him a larger fleet and an army of 9000 men. His next victory would be even more spectacular than Porto Bello.

Of all the Washingtons, the one who was most excited about the War of Jenkins's Ear was Lawrence. As soon as he heard that the army would include a regiment of men recruited in the colonies, he rushed to apply for a commission as one of its officers.

It took a while to get the American Regiment organized, but eventually Lawrence's company sailed out of Chesapeake Bay to join Admiral Vernon's fleet in Jamaica. From there, they would sail south and attack Cartagena, a busy port on the northern coast of Colombia.

Weeks passed and there was no further news. No one knew whether the assault on Cartagena had begun or ended. The Washingtons' main concern was Lawrence. Was he all right? Why hadn't they heard from him? What was going on?

It was impossible not to worry, especially after the rumors began drifting back from the Caribbean. The sailors who arrived in Fredericksburg from the West Indies reported that the British attack had been a disaster.

Could it be true?

No, of course not, everyone decided. Why should anyone believe what one sailor heard from another sailor who probably heard it from another sailor who might have made it up in the first place? Still, it was always possible that something *had* gone wrong.

A few weeks later, they discovered that everything had. Instead of racking up another great victory, Admiral Vernon had suffered a dreadful defeat.

But there was still no word from Lawrence. Then one day a letter arrived. The address was in Lawrence's handwriting. At least he was still alive and well enough to write. His father's fingers trembled as he broke open the seal and unfolded the letter.

Yes, Lawrence was fine, thank God, but he was furious about the defeat at Cartagena. Admiral Vernon was still a brilliant commander; it was the leader of the army, General Thomas Wentworth, who had messed things up.

The Admiral wanted to make a surprise attack. That had been the key to his victory at Porto Bello. But when they got within sight of Cartagena, General Wentworth decided his men weren't ready. They needed more time to unload their supplies and build fortifications.

By the time the British troops were ready, the Spaniards were, too. They mowed down most of General Wentworth's men with their muskets and cannons. An epidemic of yellow fever finished off the rest.

What angered Lawrence almost as much as the general's short-sightedness was his refusal to let the American Regiment go ashore. They weren't as well-trained as his British regulars, he claimed, and he didn't trust them under fire.

Lawrence's letter had been sent from Jamaica, where Admiral Vernon's fleet and the remnants of General Wentworth's army had retreated. They were awaiting word from the War Office on what to do next.

Word finally arrived and the answer was: nothing. The War of Jenkins's Ear was over; the American Regiment was being disbanded, and Lawrence was coming home.

"Hooray!"

That may not have been exactly what the Washingtons shouted, but it must have been something very close. It was too bad the English had been defeated. It was too bad so many men had been killed. But wasn't it great that Lawrence was all right and would soon be back in Virginia?

The Washingtons had two homecomings that summer. Shortly before Lawrence returned from Jamaica,

George's other half-brother, Austin, returned from Appleby.

While Austin was trying to catch up on everything that had been happening at Ferry Farm, George was quizzing him just as intently about Appleby. Don't think for a minute he'd forgotten about wanting to go there. If anything, he was more eager than ever. Lawrence and Austin had been eleven and twelve when they went away to school. George was ten. Only one more birthday to go.

It had already been decided that Austin would move into the Washingtons' old house in Westmoreland County, and divide his time between running that farm and helping out at the ironworks. Lawrence would be returning to Epsewasson, but first he'd have to spend a few days at Ferry Farm so his family could hear about his adventures.

Everyone gathered in front of the fireplace to listen. Lawrence described the attack on Cartagena so vividly that George could practically see the blazing guns and deadly cannonballs, and the brave men charging into battle.

Although Lawrence had been forced to watch the

action from the deck of a man-of-war, he hadn't been out of danger. The Spaniards had a battery of guns trained on the harbor and they bombarded Admiral Vernon's fleet whenever they got the chance.

Lawrence would never deny that war was a dangerous business — he was lucky to have come home in one piece — but he also found it very exciting. If there were another war, Lawrence would sign up in a minute. If George were old enough, he would too.

After awhile Lawrence announced that he'd been

doing enough of the talking. Let someone else take the floor and tell him what had been happening at Epsewasson.

Plenty, his father said.

Remember how he'd predicted that someday people would live along the upper Potomac? Well, they finally were. And not just any people either. Lawrence's new neighbor was none other than Colonel William Fairfax, one of the richest and most important men in Virginia. He had built himself a splendid mansion

called Belvoir on a point of land only a few miles below Epsewasson.

The Colonel had made most of his money by serving as land agent for his cousin, Lord Thomas Fairfax, who lived in England. Lord Fairfax owned the Fairfax Proprietary, a stretch of land that was part of Virginia but was actually big enoughto be a colony all by itself. Colonel Fairfax earned a fee every time he sold or leased a piece of it.

By now, George was getting old enough to understand why the grownups talked so much about land. Owning it was the surest way to get rich. As more and more settlers kept coming to Virginia, the price of land was going up, up, up.

At the rate the colony was growing, even a tract way back near the Blue Ridge Mountains would someday be valuable. The man who bought a few acres now could earn a steady income by leasing them and make a good profit later on if he wanted to sell.

With Lawrence and Austin home and settled, life at Ferry Farm returned to normal. George was still going to the Rev. Mr. Marye's school. He was studying geography and history and grammar, and was beginning to learn some Greek and Latin. His favorite subject, though, was mathematics.

He had breezed through addition, subtraction and multiplication and had gone on to master long division and fractions. It wouldn't be long before he was tackling algebra and geometry.

What was he going to do with his gift for figures?

George had no idea. Then one day he and his brother Samuel were rummaging through one of the storage sheds in the yard at Ferry Farm. (The sheds were the closest thing the Washingtons had to closets which didn't exist back then.)

The backyard sheds were full of odds and ends — old washtubs, iron pots, bolts of cheap cloth that were used to make clothes for the slaves. Nothing very interesting, the two boys decided, but that was before George went back for a second look.

Tucked away in a far corner, behind a broken spinning wheel and a discarded butter churn, he spied a wooden tripod. Beside it lay a long chain, a dusty telescope, and a leather box containing a collection of odd-looking instruments.

What were they? George asked his father that evening.

Surveying tools was the answer. Augustine Washington had used them as a young man.

How did they work?

Well, the chain was used for measuring boundary lines. The telescope, which had a compass at its base, was used to make sure the lines were straight and to tell how many degrees to the north or south and east or west they ran.

Once a surveyor had taken all his measurements, he could calculate the exact size and location of a piece of property. The next step was to draw a map of it. That's where the other instruments came in.

In a place like Virginia where people were always buying and selling land, surveying was an important profession. How else would people know where a parcel began and ended and whether it had the precise number of acres recorded in its deed?

George had often seen surveyors at work but he had never understood how they did their calculations. It was rather complicated, his father explained. You had to know something about mathematics.

How much?

About as much as George would know by the time he finished school. Would he like to be a surveyor?

George wasn't sure.

No matter, his father said. He was still young. There was plenty of time to make up his mind.

Since his return from the Caribbean, Lawrence had become a prominent man in the colony. Because of his experience as an army officer, the Royal Governor had appointed him Adjutant of Virginia.

The adjutant was the commander of the militia units that were the colony's standing army. Every county had its own unit and every white male between the ages of 21 and 60 had to serve in it.

Lawrence was also involved in a couple of other projects. He was enlarging the house at Epsewasson — which he had rechristened Mount Vernon, in honor of his hero, Admiral Vernon — and he was courting

Colonel William Fairfax's daughter, Nancy. That
didn't leave much time for visits from his younger
brother, but George understood. Besides, he had a
second second home.

There was a whole collection of Washington rela-
tives — aunts, uncles and cousins — who lived along
the lower Potomac in an area called Chotank. Several
of the cousins were around George's age and whenever
they all had some time off from school, they'd pester
their mothers to have him over.

One day in the spring of 1743, about two months
after his eleventh birthday, George went riding off to
Chotank. As usual, his cousins rushed out to greet
him. George scarcely had time to dismount from his
horse and brush the dust off his clothes before they
were organizing a game of *Follow the Leader*.

The next few days were crammed with good times.
George and his cousins flew kites and pitched quoits.
They went racing across the meadows and did cart-
wheels on the lawn. They played ball and badminton,
lotto and loo. Occasionally they quarreled and threat-
ened to punch each other — that's only normal — but
most of the time, they got along fine.

George was playing in the fields with his cousins one

afternoon when Samson, the slave who had accompanied him to Chotank, came riding up. George was puzzled. Surely Samson hadn't come to collect him. He'd only just arrived.

One look at the expression on Samson's face and George knew he was bringing bad news. Sure enough.

"Your mother sent me to fetch you," Samson announced. "Your father is very sick."

George returned to find the house at Ferry Farm quieter than he could ever remember. His mother was trying not to cry. Betty, Samuel, Jack and Charles looked frightened. Lawrence and Austin had been sent for but all they could do was pace the floor and shake their heads.

The doctor had diagnosed George's father's illness as gout of the stomach — whatever that was. Doctors knew very little about medicine in those days so it could have been almost anything from a heart attack to a ruptured appendix.

One thing was certain: there was no hope. George's father had signed his will and said his prayers. A day or so later he died and his body was carried back to Westmoreland County and buried in the Washington family graveyard.

For the next few weeks George was in a daze. He couldn't believe he wasn't going to walk into the drawing room some evening and find his father sitting in his favorite armchair paging through the *Virginia Gazette*.

George had never spent as much time as he would have liked with his father. Between the ironworks and the farm, Augustine Washington was always so busy. That made George even sadder because now he would never have the chance.

At the same time, George couldn't help worrying about himself. His mother still thought he needed to be minded every minute. With his father gone, who was going to tell her he didn't?

Ordinarily, George would have turned to Lawrence for help but at the moment, Lawrence had his mind on other things. He and Nancy Fairfax were going to be married in July.

The wedding took place at Belvoir which looked even more splendid than usual for the occasion. The chandeliers sparkled; the furniture gleamed; there were vases of fresh flowers in every room.

George had been afraid he'd feel out of place among the Fairfaxes and their elegant friends but Colonel Fairfax — of all people — put him at ease. The Colonel liked young people — even gawky eleven-year-olds — and went out of his way to talk to George and make him feel at home.

As the summer wore on, the Washingtons slowly adjusted to getting along without a husband and a father. There are always ten million things to be done on a farm, so George's mother had no time to sit around feeling sorry for herself. The one thing she still had time for, though, was worrying about George.

Where was he going? What was he doing? It was hot, didn't he want a mug of cold cider? It was cool, shouldn't he put on his coat?

Mary Washington's own parents had died when she was young so maybe she was giving her oldest son the kind of attention she would have enjoyed at his age. That didn't matter to George. He was tired of being treated like a two-year-old.

On top of that he had another worry. With his father dead, what were his chances of going to Appleby? He'd been dreaming of it for as long as he could remember. But if his mother was uneasy every time he took the ferry to Fredericksburg, would she ever let him sail all the way to England?

When George finally got up the nerve to ask her,

she shook her head. Surely he could get as much education as he needed right there in Virginia.

George disagreed, and Lawrence and Austin backed him up. It wasn't just the education, they insisted, it was the chance to acquire some polish and style and make friends who might be helpful later on.

Mary Washington still shook her head. George waited a while then asked her again. This time, her answer was a very definite no. She couldn't afford it. With his father dead, there wasn't enough money for luxuries.

Lawrence had been one of the executors of their father's estate so he knew that wasn't true. Although Mary Washington liked to think of herself as a poor widow, she was actually quite well off. She could have sent George to Appleby if she wanted to, but she obviously didn't want to.

Maybe you know how it feels to discover that something you've been thinking about and wishing and hoping and praying would happen isn't going to. If so, you know how George felt — AWFUL.

To make matters worse, school was in session so he couldn't cheer himself up with a visit to Mount Vernon or Chotank. He had to stay right there at Ferry Farm.

George spent a good part of the next term moping. When the Rev. Mr. Marye rang the bell for recess, George was the only one who didn't bolt for the door. He stayed at his desk, hunched over his copy book, working out problems in arithmetic. His classmates may have found that odd, but they probably didn't say so. Only an idiot would risk a fight with the strongest boy in the school.

George was about fourteen when he stopped going to school. He'd learned as much as the Rev. Mr. Marye could teach him. If he wanted to know more, he could study on his own.

With no more school to worry about, George could stay at Mount Vernon for weeks on end. He and Lawrence still went for early morning rides around the plantation and still talked about everything under the sun.

Although they were both interested in a great many subjects, Lawrence's favorite was land. He always had his eye on some parcel that would be worth a fortune someday. When they visited Nancy's folks at Belvoir, the talk was exactly the same.

Virginia was still growing. Each new wave of settlers was being forced to move further and further inland. They had already reached the foothills of the Blue Ridge Mountains. It was only a matter of time before they started trekking over the mountains and settling in the Shenandoah Valley.

Everyone agreed that the Shenandoah Valley was the smart place to buy land. The only question was: who had the right to sell it? The Royal Governor of Virginia thought the entire valley belonged to the King of England. Colonel Fairfax's cousin, Lord Thomas Fairfax, said, "No, it doesn't. It belongs to me."

The argument was finally referred to His Majesty's Privy Council in London. Amazingly enough, they agreed with Lord Fairfax. After studying all the records, they ruled that the Fairfax Proprietary not only included the Shenandoah Valley but extended over one whole section of the Allegheny Mountains into what is now the state of West Virginia.

You can be sure there was a great deal of rejoicing at Belvoir when the news reached Virginia. The Fairfaxes were going to be even richer than they already were.

There must have been a few chortles at Mount Vernon too. Lawrence had been planning to buy some tracts in the Shenandoah Valley. With his father-in-law in charge of the sales, he'd have no trouble getting them at a good price. It wouldn't be long before Lawrence was rich, too.

And what about George? He'd love to have enough money to buy land in the Shenandoah Valley, but he had no idea where to get it. Under the terms of his father's will, Ferry Farm would be his on his twenty-first birthday. Its crops would bring in enough to support him, but not enough to make him rich. Did Lawrence have any ideas?

As a matter of fact, he did. Lawrence had been giving quite a bit of thought to his half-brother's future. He wondered how George would feel about going to sea.

Lawrence didn't have to say any more. George's eyes were dancing with excitement. What a marvelous idea! He could become a midshipman in the Royal Navy and maybe someday he'd be an admiral like Edward Vernon. Wouldn't that be fantastic?

Yes, it would, Lawrence agreed, but unfortunately, the British Navy preferred native-born Englishmen rather than colonials. Lawrence's plan was for George to sign on as a cabin boy on a merchant vessel. From there he could work his way up to second mate, then first mate, and eventually, captain. Most captains owned their own ships and got a hefty cut on the cargoes they carried.

George was too thrilled with the idea of going to sea to care what kind of ship he sailed on. He was already dreaming of voyages to London and the West Indies when Lawrence brought him up short. There was one small problem: he couldn't become a cabin boy without his mother's permission.

Would she give it?

Lawrence thought she might.

Mary Washington was less of a worry-wart now that George was in his teens, but she had become stubborn and unpredictable and had to be handled with care. The best approach, the two brothers decided, would be for George to ask her first. If that didn't work, Lawrence would step in.

George brought up the subject as soon as he got back to Ferry Farm. His mother wasn't very enthusiastic about the idea, but she promised to think about it.

Weeks passed and Mary Washington was still thinking about it. Finally, George got tired of waiting. He sent Lawrence a message that said, in effect, "HELP!"

A day or two later, a messenger knocked on the door of Ferry Farm. Colonel William Fairfax was over in Fredericksburg on business, he reported, and he was carrying a pair of letters for Master George Washington. Could Master Washington come over and get them?

The letters Colonel Fairfax was carrying were from Lawrence. One was addressed to Mary Washington and contained a long list of reasons why George should go to sea. The other was for George, telling him not to be afraid to stand up to his mother and, above all, not to let her know that he and Lawrence were in cahoots.

Colonel Fairfax also carried some words of advice from Lawrence: George was not to tell his mother about his own letter and he was to wait until she was in a good mood before delivering hers.

For a boy who supposedly never told a lie, George didn't have a qualm about following Lawrence's instructions. He pretended to know nothing about the letter he passed along to his mother and acted as if it couldn't possibly have anything to do with him.

Lawrence had made out a good case for letting George go to sea but Mary Washington still wasn't convinced. She'd have to think about it a while longer.

More weeks passed while George twitched and fid-
geted and his mother wavered back and forth. There
were days when she seemed to like the idea and other
days when she acted as if it were the worst thing she'd
ever heard of. George's hopes rose and fell like the
tides in the Rappahannock.

George refused to give up. Perhaps it was because
Lawrence had told him to stand firm or perhaps he had
simply inherited his mother's stubborness. He kept
after her until she finally announced that she would
settle the matter once and for all by writing to her half-
brother, Joseph Ball, who lived in England. If he
approved, George could go to sea. If not, she didn't
want to hear another word about it.

George remembered his Uncle Joseph. He had lived
in Virginia for several years before he moved to
England. George recalled him as a kindly man who
took as much interest in his half-sister's family as he
did in his own.

Lawrence, who had visited Joseph Ball during his
years at Appleby, had a different view. Ball was still
the kindly uncle George remembered, but he had also
become rather cranky and opinionated. If he were in
George's shoes, Lawrence said, he wouldn't get his
hopes up.

George had already missed out on one thing he badly wanted — the chance to go to Appleby. Now it looked as if he were going to miss out on another. It wasn't fair!

Lawrence agreed but, fair or not, that's the way things were and there wasn't anything either one of them could do about it. It might be smarter for George to stop grumbling and start thinking about how he could earn some money if he didn't go to sea.

George already knew the answer. It was right there, in one of the storage sheds at Ferry Farm. He went out and took another look at his father's surveying instruments. He set up the tripod and peered through the telescope. He had only a vague idea of what surveyors looked for but it wouldn't be hard to find out.

Mary Washington had written to her half-brother in December. It was almost six months before she received a reply.

Sailors weren't well paid or well treated, Joseph Ball wrote, and even if George got to be master of his own ship, he wasn't likely to get rich. He'd make more money as a planter, no matter how few acres he had. In his Uncle Joseph's opinion, young George would "better be put apprentice to a tinker."

As far as Mary Washington was concerned, her half-brother was a wise man who always gave her good advice. It would have been useless to tell her that, in this case, he didn't know what he was talking about.

Thanks to Lawrence's warning, George wasn't as disappointed as he might have been. He had no intention of becoming an apprentice to a tinker — gentlemen's sons didn't go around mending kettles and pots — but there was nothing to stop him from becoming an apprentice to a surveyor. Lawrence or Colonel Fairfax were bound to know one who'd take him on.

7

George spent the next few months learning to measure land and draw maps. He tramped through woods and fields at the side of a master surveyor and did his homework by making surveys of Austin's orchards and Lawrence's turnip patch.

George liked surveying. It gave him a chance to use the mathematics he'd learned in school and to work outdoors — which he much preferred to being cooped up inside. Best of all, he no longer had to sit and listen when the conversations at Mount Vernon or Belvoir turned to land. Now he could join right in.

The Shenandoah Valley was still a long way from being completely settled but Lawrence was already

looking forward to the day when people would venture even farther west — to Ohio, for instance. There were millions and millions of acres out there just waiting to be cleared and farmed.

In the summer of 1747, there was a lull in the talk about land. The new topic of conversation was the arrival from London of Lord Thomas Fairfax. He was going to stay at Belvoir and everyone, including George, was hoping for a chance to meet him.

George had never seen a lord before. As his horse trotted up the road to Belvoir, he tried to imagine what His Lordship would be like. Very dignified, he decided, with perfect manners and clothes cut in the latest London fashion.

George was sure his own best coat and breeches would look shabby next to Lord Fairfax's outfit, but he could at least be proud of his manners. He knew better than to spit in the fire or pick his teeth or forget to stand up when His Lordship entered the room.

Two years earlier George had found a book called *Youth's Behavior* which contained several dozen Rules of Civility designed to turn boorish boys into polite young men. He had copied the rules in a notebook and had tried to follow them ever since. There was nothing he hated more than making a fool of himself in public.

Having arrived at Belvoir expecting to meet a stylishly dressed nobleman, George was surprised to find himself being introduced to a man who could have passed for a backwoods farmer. Lord Fairfax's clothes were old and rumpled and not very clean, and he looked as if he hadn't washed his face or combed his hair in days.

If Lord Fairfax had ever read the Rules of Civility, he certainly didn't follow them. He was rude to most of the men he met, and even ruder to the women. He refused to talk to them unless he absolutely had to.

As you can imagine, Lord Fairfax wasn't the most charming house guest in the world but the Fairfaxes couldn't complain. They wouldn't be as rich as they were if His Lordship hadn't made the Colonel his land agent.

By now George was a regular visitor at Belvoir. He felt very much at home with the Fairfaxes and he was particularly fond of their son, George William. Mr. Fairfax, as George called him, was seven years older than he was but they'd become friends just the same.

George could spend an entire day at Belvoir and barely see His Lordship. He was usually holed up in the Colonel's study poring over maps of his proprietary and trying to figure out which tracts to sell next.

Lord Fairfax had selected a section in a far corner of the Shenandoah Valley. At the moment it was too remote to attract settlers but that wouldn't last. His Lordship wanted it surveyed without delay.

George happened to be at Belvoir when Lord Fairfax and the Colonel were discussing the matter. They'd already hired a surveyor, and George William Fairfax was going along as His Lordship's representative. Suddenly Colonel Fairfax turned to George.

"The surveyor could use an assistant," he said. "Would you like to go, too?"

Would he! He could hardly wait to get started.

By now, George thought he was old enough not to

have to ask for his mother's permission but, just to be on the safe side, he did. A messenger was sent galloping off to Ferry Farm with a note for Mary Washington. By some miracle — or perhaps she was just in a good mood that day — her answer was yes.

George's trip to the Shenandoah Valley was the greatest adventure of his sixteen years. For the first time in his life, he slept outdoors and cooked his own meals over a campfire. He met people who were totally different from the ones he knew back home — bearded frontiersmen who wore deerskin shirts and told time by the sun, German settlers who couldn't speak English, even a band of Indians all decked out in warpaint and

feathers. (Fortunately, they turned out to be friendlier than they looked.)

Surveying in the wilderness wasn't easy — the grass was taller, the woods were thicker and there was always a risk of meeting rattlesnakes or bears. But traveling in the wilderness was even worse. The trails were so rocky and rutted it was a miracle their horses didn't stumble and throw them to the ground. To add to their problems, it rained almost the whole time they were gone so their clothes were always soggy and their boots squishy with mud.

There weren't any inns in the Shenandoah Valley, and there certainly weren't any motels. Sometimes they found a farmer to take them in, but the accommodations weren't always clean or comfortable. In one place dinner was served on a bare table without a sign of a knife and fork. In another, their host made them sleep on straw mats that were crawling with bedbugs and fleas.

Nevertheless, George enjoyed everything about the trip — except the bedbugs and fleas. It gave him a chance to see the Shenandoah Valley (Lawrence and Austin may have gone to school in England but neither one of them had done *that*) and to find out something about himself.

With slaves to do most of the work, life was soft at Ferry Farm and Mount Vernon. But George didn't want to be soft; he wanted to be tough. After spending thirty-three days in the wilderness without a moment of whining or complaining or wishing he could turn around and go home, he decided that he was.

8

Now that he'd actually seen the Shenandoah Valley, George was more anxious than ever to buy land there. It wouldn't always be a wilderness. In another five or ten years, the frontier cabins would be replaced by honest-to-goodness farmhouses, the trails would become roads, and the meadows and forests, neatly plowed fields.

If anyone doubted it, all they had to do was look at the upper Potomac. When George was a little boy, nobody wanted to live there because it was too far out of the way. Then property on the lower Potomac became harder and harder to come by and people changed their minds.

By 1744 the area was large enough to become a county — Fairfax — and five years later, the county was large enough to have a town. It was going to be built on sixty acres of land about ten miles up the Potomac from Mount Vernon. The site was called Belhaven but it's name would be changed to Alexandria.

The Fairfax County surveyor was in charge of laying out the streets and measuring off the lots for the new town but since its founders included no less than three Fairfaxes — His Lordship, the Colonel and George William — guess who was hired to help him?

Two weeks after he handed in his survey maps of Alexandria, George became a county surveyor himself. The county, Culpepper, was in another rapidly growing area along the Rappahannock River, about thirty miles above Fredericksburg.

As county surveyor, George was responsible for all the surveys that were made in Culpepper County, but he was also free to accept commissions anywhere in the colony. Once, Lord Fairfax hired him to survey some tracts in the Shenandoah Valley.

Although George had enjoyed his first trip to the wilderness, he didn't enjoy his second. For one thing, there was no Mr. Fairfax for company. For another, it was November and the weather was horrendously cold and raw.

George slept with all his clothes on but no matter how close he huddled to the fire or how tightly he wrapped his bearskin blanket around him, he never felt warm. The only good part of the trip, he decided, would be the stop at Belvoir to collect his fee.

His Lordship would probably growl at him — his manners hadn't improved — but after he delivered his survey maps, he could look forward to a pleasant visit with Mr. Fairfax and his new bride, Sally.

George had never been good at talking to girls. He was forever stumbling over his words or saying something stupid, but Sally's cheerful smile and friendly manner made his shyness disappear. She was only two years older than he was and, although he never would have said so out loud, George couldn't help wishing he had found her first.

Mr. Fairfax had met Sally in Williamsburg when he was attending one of the sessions of the House of Burgesses, the elected body that helped make the laws for the colony. Lawrence was also a member of the House of Burgesses, but lately he hadn't felt well enough to go. He was bothered by a wracking cough and spells of weakness and fever that lasted for most of the winter.

When spring came, Lawrence began to feel better, and by summer he was completely cured and on his way to London. The main purpose of the trip was to see about getting the rights to some land in Ohio, which he could then turn around and sell; but while he was there, he also planned to consult a doctor about his illness.

The doctor wasn't very helpful. He had no idea what the trouble was or how to cure it, but Lawrence came home in high spirits anyway. He had succeeded in getting a royal grant of 200,000 acres in Ohio. King George II wanted to encourage settlements there. A fort or two flying the British flag might stop the French from sneaking down from Canada and trying to claim the land for France.

Lawrence was planning to set up an Ohio company to handle the sales of his land grant. When it was organized, George could do some of the surveys. In the meantime, he had more than enough work to keep him busy.

Surveying paid well — which was another reason George liked it. Within a year after his appointment as Culpepper County surveyor, he had saved enough money to buy three parcels of land in the Shenandoah Valley — 1,459 acres all told. It was only a speck compared to what Lawrence and Mr. Fairfax owned but it wasn't a bad start for an eighteen-year-old.

Although George worked hard, he rarely missed a chance to enjoy himself. Like most Virginians, he liked parties and picnics and barbecues and balls. At Mount Vernon, he and Lawrence went fox hunting with the Fairfaxes or duck hunting in the marshes along the Potomac. At Ferry Farm, he might challenge his younger brothers to a horse race or spend an evening at one of Fredericksburg's taverns playing billiards or cards.

In the scorching heat of a Virginia summer, there was nothing more refreshing than a nice cool swim. One day, when he was staying at Ferry Farm, George found a secluded spot along the Rappahannock, stripped off his clothes and plunged in.

When he came out of the water his clothes were still lying on the river bank where he'd left them, but when he started to get dressed he realized that someone had gone through his pockets and stolen his money.

Things could have been worse. If his clothes had been stolen George would have had to scamper home in his birthday suit. As it was, he reported the theft to the sheriff and in no time at all, two women — inden-

tured servants from Fredericksburg — were arrested and locked in the town jail.

When the case came to trial the following December, one of the women turned King's witness and testified against the other. She was found guilty of petty larceny and given the usual punishment — fifteen lashes on her bare back at the public whipping post. By that time, however, George was a thousand miles away and his mind was on other things.

Lawrence's illness had not only returned, it had gotten worse. For the first time since they'd known each other, George was worried about his older brother instead of the other way around.

Since Lawrence always felt sicker in winter, the doctor was inclined to blame the cold weather. He advised Lawrence to spend the next winter in a warmer climate.

Barbados seemed like the best place to go. It was easy to get to — there were ships sailing from Virginia to Barbados all the time — and Colonel Fairfax had a friend on the island who could find him a place to stay.

Lawrence wasn't strong enough to travel alone. Nancy wanted to go with him but she was afraid to take their ten-month-old baby, Sally, to a Caribbean island where she might be exposed to all sorts of diseases. Lawrence and Nancy had already lost three babies. They didn't want to lose a fourth.

Austin was too busy to go with Lawrence. Samuel, Jack and Charles were too young. George was the only one left. The trip would mean losing several months' worth of surveying fees but that didn't matter. Lawrence's health was more important than anything else.

The voyage to Barbados took a little over a month.
If George had been a sailor, he would have been busy
scrambling up and down the rigging and trimming the
sails. As a passenger, he was bored. He whiled away
the time by keeping a journal, and now and then he
threw a line over the side and caught some fresh fish
for dinner.

For the first few days after they landed, Lawrence
was too weak to do very much, but George set out to
explore the island. He liked the white-washed houses
with their high verandas, the fields of pineapple and
sugar cane, and the gardens blooming with tropical
flowers, but he was particularly interested in the fort

that had been built to defend Barbados against an enemy attack.

George had never seen a fort before, but nobody would have guessed it. He inspected the guns and the battlements so thoroughly, you would have thought he was a junior officer in the army.

Ironically, George went to Barbados for Lawrence's health but within two weeks of their arrival Lawrence felt better and George was the one who got sick. He came down with smallpox and almost died.

He didn't, of course, but there must have been times when he wished he would. Anything to put an end to his raging fever and horrible headache and the clusters of ugly blisters that covered his body.

George certainly didn't enjoy having smallpox — who would? — but in those days, almost everyone caught the disease at some point in their lives, and there was something to be said for getting it over with. If you survived, you'd be immune for the rest of your life.

By the time George recovered, Lawrence was feeling so much better he insisted on sending George home. He was well enough to take care of himself, and it wasn't fair to keep his brother in Barbados when there were surveying jobs waiting in Virginia.

A few days later, George booked passage on a ship that was sailing for Yorktown. The port was only twelve miles from Williamsburg and he had promised to deliver some letters from people in Barbados to Virginia's new governor, Robert Dinwiddie.

When they landed at Yorktown, George hired a horse and set out for Williamsburg. By mid-afternoon he was clopping up Duke of Gloucester Street to the Governor's Palace. Governor Dinwiddie took the letters George was carrying. Then he invited him to sit down and visit for awhile.

George was surprised. The new governor had the reputation of being rather stern but he wasn't that way with George. They chatted about this and that and before long, the governor was urging George to stay for dinner.

It was quite an honor for a twenty-year old county surveyor to be invited to dine alone with the governor but Robert Dinwiddie wanted to know more about the far reaches of his colony and George, who had been to the Shenandoah Valley, was one of the few people who could tell him. Not only that, but George and Governor Dinwiddie had something in common. The governor was a surveyor, too.

The spring after his return from Barbados, George became interested in a young lady named Betsy Fauntleroy. He called on her once but when he wrote her a note asking to see her again, she said no. She wasn't interested in Mr. Washington and he was not to come calling again.

George knew his face was slightly pockmarked and his nose was a trifle long but he didn't think he was *that* bad. On the plus side, he was tall and broad-shouldered and on his way to becoming rich. He wasn't a bad dancer either. He'd taken lessons so he'd know all the right steps.

It always hurts to be turned down by someone you like, but George didn't have time to brood about Betsy's rejection. He had another more serious worry: Lawrence was sick again.

Shortly after George left for Virginia, Lawrence got tired of Barbados and decided to move to Bermuda. He had barely arrived when his cough and fever returned. A local doctor diagnosed the problem as consumption but, with the proper treatment, he thought it might be cured.

Weeks passed and Lawrence's letters home began to sound more and more discouraged. He was doing exactly what his doctor ordered, Lawrence wrote, but he seemed to be getting worse instead of better.

Early in June, a ship sailed up the Potomac and anchored off Mount Vernon. Instead of bringing a letter from Lawrence, the ship carried Lawrence himself. He was pale and gaunt and so weak that Nancy had to send for a carriage to carry him from the wharf to the house. George took one look at his older brother and knew he had come home to die.

It was heartbreaking to watch Lawrence slipping away. He had always been so full of energy — bursting with plans for improving Mount Vernon, devising ways to acquire more land, rushing off to Williamsburg to vote on some new law or consult with the governor about the militia.

Lawrence was a real leader, a success in almost everything he tackled. Influential men, like Colonel Fairfax, considered him one of the most promising young men in the colony. Now he would never fulfill that promise.

The next few weeks were a gloomy time at Mount Vernon. Lawrence spent his days propped up in bed with Nancy or George — or both — at his side. He drew up his will, with George as the executor. Most of his property would go to Nancy and their little daughter, Sally, but if Nancy remarried and Sally died, Mount Vernon would go to George.

As the days wore on, Lawrence grew worse and finally towards the end of July, he died. It was a sad day for Nancy and little Sally but it was just as sad for George. He and Lawrence had been more than brothers, they had also been the closest of friends.

~10~

Before he went to Barbados, Lawrence had asked Governor Dinwiddie to replace him as Adjutant of Virginia. The governor had dragged his feet — perhaps he was hoping that Lawrence would recover — but now he had no choice.

If anyone had made up a list of all the men in the colony who were qualified to become adjutant, George wouldn't have been on it. He was only twenty and he had no experience as a soldier. He was too young even to serve in the militia. But that didn't stop him from writing to Governor Dinwiddie proposing himself as Lawrence's replacement.

For a young man who was normally steady and sensible, it was a brash thing to do, but George's brashness was a sign of how desperately he wanted the job. If he got it, he'd be following in Lawrence's footsteps — which he'd been trying to do for most of his life. A nod from Governor Dinwiddie and he could become a soldier, a leader and an important man in the colony — just like Lawrence.

Governor Dinwiddie didn't answer George's letter but according to Mr. Fairfax, who was always up on the news from Williamsburg, the matter was pretty well settled. The governor was planning to divide the colony into three militia districts and appoint an adjutant for each. He had already selected the three men and they were all older and more experienced than George. One had been with Lawrence at the siege of Cartagena.

George should have abandoned the idea of becoming adjutant right then and there. Clearly, he didn't stand a chance. Instead, he became brasher than ever. He wrote another letter to the governor reminding him that he was available if any of the other men couldn't serve.

Four months after Lawrence's death, Governor Dinwiddie finally got around to naming his successor. As expected, he appointed three adjutants. As *not* expected, he created a fourth militia district for the counties in the southern part of the colony. The adjutant for that district, which lay between the James River and the North Carolina border, would be none other than Lawrence Washington's younger brother, George.

It's hard to say why Governor Dinwiddie did what he did. Maybe he was impressed by George's persistence. Maybe he wanted to console him for the loss of his brother. Maybe he had sensed, during their dinner in Williamsburg, that George was an extraordinary young man. Or maybe he simply shrugged and said, "Why not give the boy a chance? There aren't that many people in the southern counties; how much harm can he do?"

George took his oath of office on February 1, 1753 — only a few weeks before his twenty-first birthday. He wore his new uniform — red breeches and a dark blue coat with brass buttons — and a sword with a silver handle was strapped to his waist. From now on, he would be known as Major Washington.

The new major didn't expect to do any fighting. His main job would be training the militia to march and obey orders. But things could always change. There might be trouble on the frontier or a flareup of the on-

again, off-again war England and France had been fighting for the control of North America.

No one could predict the future.

That's why young Major Washington had no way of knowing that he wasn't always going to be a part-time soldier and a county surveyor. Someday he'd be even more distinguished than his brother, Lawrence, and his fame would extend thousands of miles beyond Virginia. People all over the world would know him as a brilliant general and the father and president of a remarkable new country.

That George Washington wouldn't be a trim young major. He'd be a man in his sixties with grey hair and wrinkles and a bit of a paunch. Someone would paint his portrait and he'd have to look stern and dignified — famous men always did. Unfortunately, that would only make it all the harder for people to believe that this great hero had ever been a young man — or a boy — just like everyone else.

But you know he was.